Dear Diary

A Poetry Collection by
Alana Avellino

Copyright © 2025 by Alana Avellino
All rights reserved.

No part of this publication may be reproduced, distributed, or transmitted in any form or by any means, including photocopying, recording, or other electronic or mechanical methods, without the prior written permission of the publisher, except in the case of brief quotations used in critical reviews or scholarly works.
This book is a work of creative nonfiction. All poems in this collection were originally created and written by the author. For permission requests, please contact the author directly at:
alanawrites.contact@gmail.com

Cover Art: Paul Smith

First Edition
Printed in Canada

Library and Archives Canada Cataloguing in Publication
Title: *Dear Diary* / Alana Avellino
Name: Avellino, Alana, author.

ISBN: [978-1-0696762-0-7]

Canadian copyright registration number: [1235157]

For my children-
So you always know it's never too late to follow your dreams.
Reach for the stars. Always.

a note on Dear Diary ...

I have always felt things deeply, empathetically and sometimes compulsive to a degree. My thoughts turn into stories, weaving dreamlands and escapes, adventures and creations. I am both a dreamer and a realist and those parts of me have always fought against each other. Reality keeps me grounded, but dreaming sets me free. And when I allow myself to write, to create, something powerful comes alive.

For a long time, I dreamed of having one of my books out in the world- of sharing my words and connecting with others. But it wasn't until I began to believe in myself, to shift my self-concept and see my own worth, that I knew this collection was meant to be.

Dear Diary *was born from years of journaling, reflection, and surviving the messy parts of life. These poems carry pieces of my innocence, my grief, my shadows, and my becoming. They are my heart poured onto the page, written with honesty and vulnerability, some found in inspiration from the world around me. Not just as my own story, but as a mirror for anyone who has ever struggled to find the words, carried a heaviness, or hoped to find themselves again.*

You are not alone. You are not broken.
And it's never too late to become who you've always dreamed of.

dear diary,
I never meant for these pages to become a book
they were just pieces of me-
grief and hope, shadows and light,
the parts I couldn't say out loud, that I kept to myself.

But somewhere in between the breaking
and the becoming,
I realized these words weren't just mine,
they belong to anyone who has ever felt lost,
ever needed to be seen,
ever hoped to be heard.

Connection

purely from the heart
a place to start
letting judgments go
received or not
embodying flow

creating is creation
through worlds of dreams
and inspiration
listening quietly to
what you have to say
what you want to say

it is needed
is meant to be
is meant for the world to see
even in fear we forge ahead
the message finding you
again
and again

regardless of doubt
holding you back
it's not out of lack

ideas come bursting
at the seams
words blurred
unseen
unable to contain the urge
to write it out
to make it heard

...

for anyone,
for everyone

that needs to feel
needs to see
read the stories
that help them heal

to see themselves
in someone's eyes
inside their life
it feels the same
it feels like they've
experienced your pain

across the world
we're all connected
intertwined
like puzzled
pieces
finding time
searching for
more
inside this life

Table of Contents

Section One: The Wanting
    Before
    Coming of Age
    Safe
    Dear Diary
    Untrust
    Dreamy Daze
    Will They

Section Two: The Breaking
    Sixteen
    Silent Chaos
    Autopilot
    Anxiety
    Freefall
    Surrender
    Hidden

Section Three: The Mirror
    Imposter
    Words
    Choice
    Promises
    Higher Ground
    Perfection
    Mirror
    Glass Ceiling

Section Four: The Shadows
    You
    Forever
    Wasteland
    Echos
    Old Self
    Time
    Enough
    Shadows
    One by One

Section Five: The Becoming
    Listen
    Growth
    Wake up
    Seed
    Waiting
    Patience
    Miracles
    Believe
    Blessings
    Faith
    Peace
    Embers

*the magic and wonder of childhood is not a
flaw to outgrow
but a precious gift to protect*

The Wanting

A space of innocence and wonder.
Where dreams feel endless and possibility is effortless. A reminder of what it means to believe freely- before the world teaches us otherwise.

Before

Before was an innocence
a dreamscape of wonder,
a land of play,
of make-believe,
of silent ponder.

Before was youthful,
a vibrancy unmet,
a magical enchantment
of blanket forts,
no regrets.

Before was expansive,
a solar system of wishes,
a never-ending story
of adventure,
of idealism.

Before was before-
the world cracked open life.
When dreams once dreamt
and candles blown
turned happiness to strife.

When reality turned daunting,
and escapism became haunting;
and the future brought before,
before,
you learned to ask for more.

Coming of Age

Coming of age,
the world is my stage
freedom and bliss exist-
in dreams long awaited
in love that was fated.

It happens in longing wishes.

Who will I be?
Who could I be?

My heart grew with
every thought.
What I didn't know,
what I longed to know,
would soon be
what I forgot.

Safe

Thunderstorms rumbled,
quaking the night,
but fear never grazed me,
never fazed me-
there was always a place
for me to feel safe,
to hide.

The quiet of your presence
assured me, day after day
a place I called home,
a place I yearned to stay.
Stay forever, if I could,
if you would
let me.

Unconditionally loved,
regardless of faults.
A sturdy heart
that never wavered,
even now, as an adult-
A mother, *I am too*.
Learned how to
love from you.

You were never too far,
but always close enough
when times were too easy,
when life became tough

your softness exuded,
a gentle embrace-

...

A mother's touch,
you soothed my heart,
bandaged my wounds,
created a space
for me to come to.

A space I called home.
I longed to return,
where wild curiosity lay
and daydreams were learned.

The ease of joy and laughter,
a pace fueled only
by love-
of quiet understandings,
of patience above
all,
of soul-deep knowing,
of nurturing and growing,
of trusting you with all that
you knew.

I love you.

And with me, I carry all that I know.
When I hold them,
and love them,
the way you showed
me how.

alanaavellinoauthor | poetry

summer nights beneath black starlit skies
sticky hands covered in marshmallow glaze
the moon showed the way
to who I'd be someday
and I was eager to listen

Dear Diary

I want to be loved,
chosen,
and seen.

The outside is false.
Just a veil of protection
for what desires wish to be.

In love,
love,
love to be loved.

Why is it so hard to be first?
To be above,
to rise up and spread your truth-
in love.

Would eyes recognize me,
hold me that high?
The tower beneath crumbles,
perceptions fade into the night.

If I were protected,
I could be so special.
The shadows come hungry to steal,
invading all potential.

Courage is nothing without a village
questions un end the faith within,
spiraling chaos-
letting them win.

...

If I were loved,
chosen,
and seen...
I could be free.
I could be me.

Untrust

Who do you need,
if not, who you want?
And who do you want,
if what you need is always gone?

Left unmet,
unkept,
distorted in lack
wishing it back.

Questioning that inner voice:
Is it them?
Is it you?
Forgoing the part
that is meant to shine through.

Games on games,
heartbreak at most.
Rooted in disease,
trust no one sees.

In the shadows,
behind fake smiles,
hidden in ignorance,
while pleading innocence.

Drained of life,
a circus of thoughts-
never worthy
of what you've got.

...

A mind cannot be changed
or warned.
Colours speak more
than words alone.

No apologies.
Betrayal cuts deep.
But betrayal of self-
is an unimaginable feat.

Cleanse from within.
Return to the truth.
The answers will always
lie within you.

Dreamy Daze

Dreamy daze,
summer-filled nights,
epic memories made
beneath the moonlight.

Butterflies flew
in my heart
as it grew,
as it grew-
stronger
and brighter for you.

For you,
stars shone in my eyes.
It was at this time
I never had to disguise
the truth of myself,
of what could be.
The world felt weightless,
unexpected,
free.

Will They

Will beauty be all that is seen
or is there more,
where is more,
deep within the layers of your soul?

Will they see past your smile
to what makes you smile?
Love your heart
for what makes you who you are?

Will they recognize sadness in your eyes?
Will they know what causes you pain-
and how to make it go away?

Will they love all of you, the good and bad
the weird little habits that drive them mad,
the parts of you you're scared to show?

Will they
let you
be
all that you know?
Be you,
true to who you are,
at the essence of your core.
Will they make you laugh?
Will they be the thing,
the one
you have to have-
to be free?

...

Will they make you feel safe
each and every day?
Will their arms feel like home
the only place you want to go?

Will they see your mind,
love your mind,
cherish your kindness
for eternity?
Say yes
and don't let go.

alanaavellinoauthor | poetry

*the darkest parts of ourselves
have the potential to become the
most beautiful*

The Breaking

When the ground shifts beneath us. When loss, change and fear can alter the way we see ourselves and everything around us. These are the moments that test our strength, often experienced in silence.

Sixteen

My fingers grazed the edge of the world,
the promise of life,
the unfurling of age.
Magic awaited,
one step to take.

Exploration danced in my dreams,
ruffled my limbs,
bursting at the seams-
held only for quick moments, unseen.

A new dawn,
a new day.
Only unlimited potential
stood in my way,
inviting me to stay.

The sky was the limit,
until my limit
ran out.
Until the big, bright universe
that awaited,
shutdown.

Until darkness moved in.
Until my safety fell short.
Blinded by life,
by pain,
with no fair warning.

The edge of the world moved
so far away,

...

retreating behind armor
day after day.

Suffering in silence
is how I became.
Trust in beliefs,
crumbled to dust-
trust in myself,
in you,
in them,
in everyone.

Close the doors,
block all paths.
Smile outside,
even though I am sad.

Even though I am sad,
and scared,
I don't show.
I don't dare,
be all that I know.
Tucked away neatly,
with a nice little bow.

Set into motion,
a new way of being,
a new way of seeing,
a new way of living-
if living is grieving.

Cover myself in pretty clothes
be who I need to be
to those…

...

to those who need
a nice, happy girl,
a girl that wishes
for the entire world.

A world that no longer makes sense
That robbed me of all innocence.
That scorched the magic in my heart,
now…
where am I supposed to start?

Silent Chaos

It begins with a flutter,
a sense of unease,
until your world becomes weightless-
no longer rooted,
buckling you at the knees.

A creeping sensation litters your skin,
crawling through the places within,
gnawing and aching,
begging to give in.

Unwanted images leak into your mind,
looping fears with desires,
becoming unhinged-
devouring the torment of never ending time.

You can wish it to stop,
pray to be free,
sell your soul for a bargain-
but a body blinded by fear

is too broken to see

It's silent in the chaos ripping you apart.
It comes unattended,
when moments are unexpected-
stoic on the outside,
but thunder in your heart.

It shows its colors
whenever it pleases,

...

finding the weakness
that is no longer dormant,
striking with power.
It isn't made up
this is a disease.

When the battle ends,
a withered body remains-
empty and breathless,
mind, body, and soul…
lifeless.

A brief reprieve
until it crawls back.
Until you're happy.
Until you're sad.
Until it seeks you out once more,
when silent chaos
comes knocking
on your door.

AutoPilot

You work so hard,
but you're unhappy.
You work too hard,
and life forgets you.

Moves on without you,
moves up and forward.
Forging along-
while you stay stuck,
beaten from burden.

What is it for?
If you're not here-
Who is it for?
If no one's watching-
Why does it matter?
If you're not living.

Life doesn't wait,
time doesn't stop.
And lessons are taught,
once it's too late.

When your body is broken,
and your mind is tired.
Your heart is sore,
and your soul is crying.

Anxiety

Can't breathe,
can't see
invisible ropes
threaten beneath.

Binding tight,
they squeeze the life.

Shoulders rise,
in disguise
to hide a shallow inhale.

But there's no relief
or reprieve-
uneasiness quickens
to no avail.

Attention to detail,
but the wrong detail in mind.
Focusing on broken parts
is wasting time.

Time that slows
as anxiety grows,
as your body struggles
and continues to show-

Show you that you're giving in,
allowing your fears
and worries to win.

...

Unrealistic and relentless,
as you allow it to take
what it wants-
to finish
what it came for.
You.

Freefall

You want to let go,
be free,
experience life the way
everyone else sees
it.

But you don't believe
it's safe
not really-
for good things
to happen,
to come your way.

Too many ups
must come with a down.
When you're climbing to the top,
free falling,
afraid you'll lose your crown.

It's a story,
a tale-
that's turned you into
a frail
shell of who you were meant to be.

A lie
you live by,
a secret you give.
A fear set in its ways,
from the days

...

you lost
and the cost
of its pain.

It's a lack mindset
you live in.

*sometimes healing
is impossible
when survival
becomes inevitable*

Surrender

Sometimes we just want to feel
the hurt,
the ache,
rumbling beneath the surface.

To feel
is to heal,
powerful in its wake.
Make no mistake-
it's not an easy feat.

But days when gloomy
makes an appearance,
there is no difference
in where you are.
Tidal waves of life are never far.

So closed off,
unable to grow,
too afraid to show
the darkness that feeds
on your insecurities.

But darkness is where freedom lay.
Surrendering to fear-
pull back the curtain,
crawl through the webs
it's the only true way to heal.

Hidden

It's hidden in the smiles
that hold a shallow grave,
in the empty eyes and forceful
laugh,
in the guilt that tells you
it's not enough.

In the coping
that isn't coping,
in the pain that's dulled
by hoping.

You believe,
so I believe-
and the circle of lies continues
to weave.

*The mirror doesn't always tell the truth
reflections are only skin deep
it will feed you lies
till the hate outside
becomes the only thing you see*

The Mirror

When self-reflection meets self-doubt. When the stories we've believed about ourselves begin to blur and we're left to question who we are, what we're worth, and what it means to truly be seen.

Imposter

It can be hard living in this space-
emptiness spilling,
filling your cup,
hollowness a slow bleed
into the places that ache.

Smiling with tired muscles,
hiding the quiet within,
the truth that wants to speak,
the lies that always win.

Yearning for the idea of what others see.
Be who you know-
but the mirror puts on a different show.

There is no rhyme or reason,
no way to understand.
Bury yourself under covers,
Praying for a plan.

A plan to go back to before.
But "before" is another life,
another time,
another closed door.

Words

Words are just words-
until they hold
truth.
Until they speak weight,
humbling the monster within you.

A symphony of creation,
evoking inspiration,
left meaningless in the wrong hands,
only to blossom in another.

They evoke flow
saying things you didn't feel,
didn't mean,
didn't know.

They move your heart, and haunt your life,
nestling in the undercarriage of your mind,
finding the empty space
invisible to the naked eye.

Hollow out feeling,
transform one's meaning.
The power to reroute a path
good or bad.

Words are just words,
until they're not.
Until we give them what they want.

alanaavellinoauthor | poetry

Promises

Promises we make
we take
for granted

life flows by-
in time,
it fades

yet we
remain:
a truth
or a lie

Choice

A circle inside
trapped behind
clawing,
scraping,
screaming to be seen.

You want out.
To be set free,
to be rid of the lies
kept in
captivity.

Burning deep,
suppressing down,
afraid of words
and prying eyes.
Afraid to bare your soul.
Afraid for the world to know.

Beliefs have you
in a choke hold.

Imposter syndrome
louder than life-
suppressing your true hearts goal,
fears cut like a knife.

Frozen in a dream,
of who you used to be,
of who you longed to be.

...

If you were brave,
if you were strong,
if it were as easy as claiming
your voice…
as if there was a choice.

Higher Ground

I'm not afraid
of what's inside,
what's to hide?
what's a lie?

Accountability.
There has never been
a voice of perfection.

I am higher ground.
I see the past
through reflection.

Perfection

Your perfection
isn't her perfection,
isn't what determines
your worth.

To be perfect
is imperfect-
isn't worth it, isn't real.
Perfectionism is a mindset
that doesn't see past the veil,
set in stone
to those unable to heal.

Perfect
is an idea,
a thought,
an image we're taught
to believe.

What's perfect in one
isn't perfect in two-
what does perfection
mean to you?

What makes you different
makes you *you*.
It's what is
to be seen through.
Through the eyes
of the beholder
grow bolder,
stand in your light.

...

Be strong within-
a strength that grows
inside,
shows
outside.

doubt used to scare me
pull me away from myself
now I see it for what it is
a coward
because without my power
it's helpless

Mirror

Is there enough space to hold-
to receive all of my blessings?
What's meant for me
do I believe
I deserve
it all.

For granted wishes
and dreams once prayed,
keeping the faith,
believing it's possible-
even on hard days.

On days when doubt
invades my mind,
where words scream louder
true, untrue,
unkind.

Feeling small in the grand scheme
of it all.
Tiredness creeps in the battlefield
of thoughts.
Giving up seems effortless
until it's not,
until it's the one thing you *cannot* do.
Until the only thing
is to push through.

Silence the ego
shut out the world,
remember the dreams
of that little girl-

...

Of the little girl who trusted
she could.

Look in the mirror and
say: *I can.*
She would.

Glass Ceiling

There's a ceiling made of glass,
and on the other side is life.
The clouds are made of heaven
the air is free
and it calls to you
at night.

The stars shine even brighter,
in the never-ending sky.
It dangles dreams above your head
yet still, you run and hide.

In bravery, you try and imagine
there could be a way out.
You touch your hand to the cold-
glass cracks beneath your palm,
and destiny unfolds.

Inside you feel the sliver,
the catastrophe
of it breaking.
you lay back down in fear
of the mistake you could be making.

The imprint of your fingertips
stares down at you
taunting
On the other side lays your potential
everything you've ever wanted.
Time only tells if you'll rise
to the occasion.

...

Or if you'll spend your life
staring through the glass
at everything you're missing.

*we cannot expect wounds to heal
if we only treat the surface layer*

The Shadows

In the shadows we find the quiet places we avoid. The weight we sometimes carry in secret. Here, we meet the parts of ourselves we've outgrown, memories that haunt us, and fears we've kept hidden- but also a strength that rises when we're finally ready to face them.

You

The memory fades-
becomes harder to place,
to face.

But a safety remains.
Only now can I understand:
the hole left in your absence
was meant to push me,
through resistance.

To be resilient.
To be brilliant.

Pain never comes
without peace.
A tunnel with no light
until we choose to see.
I can go back,
when I try.
Close my eyes
and breathe.

I see you-
in your chair,
sitting on your lap,
the blue of your eyes shine

I hear your laugh,
the smell of cigar,
in the home that was yours,
but still felt like mine.

...

It feels too big to miss you,
to remember the way you left,
to wonder why it all happened-

To question life
as a gift.

To live in a world
that now felt so wrong,
to become scared
of every single thing.

It felt like a lie.
Like another life.
It felt like an ache
that made me want to die.

But not die-
because the fear was so tangible,
entangled
in every new moment,
in every new day-
dirtying the water,
soiling my heart,
and making me this way:

Afraid.

Forever

Is it true
that nothing lasts forever?
in the stages of happiness
or the pages of grief-
we reap what we sow,
we sow what we reap.

If nothing lasts forever,
does forever
ever end?
Is there completion?
An edge of deletion?
Or does it blossom
from something old,
to something new-
something used?

If forever is never-ending,
if waiting is a game of time,
who do we lean on?
How do we know that we'll be fine,
that we'll survive?

This too shall pass.
Pass the time with distractions-
interactions,
practice patience.

...

If patience was real.
If distractions worked
to eliminate how you feel.

Wait it out
until the endlessness of time
ceases to exist-
until everything hinges
on one simple wish.

Wasteland

Paralyzed by fear
for so many years-
a magic thief
that grows from your grief,
While you remain stuck-
out of luck.

A valley of quicksand
in the dream wasteland,
battling perseverance
while too scared to stop.

Too scared to lean in,
to let in the truth-
A mindset deluded
and muted-
with a truth and a lie
every time that you try,
sabotaging life's
very beauty.

Echos

Echos
sing in the past,
linger in the present,
haunt what's to come,
the future becoming distant.

Echos
of me-
of what was,
the stranger I once was
or used to be.

They are just noise,
the song of a choice,
a version collapsed,
reversing your voice.

Echos chase you,
as fear tries to replace you,
a windchime of memories,
words kept private
in diaries.

Actions ignored,
decisions never made-
echos are ripples of life
that eventually fade.
They can be beautiful,
if you let them,
they can be kind,
if you choose.

...

Echos come and go,
as you move through-
you.

alanaavellinoauthor | poetry

Old Self

There was always potential,
but weakness preyed in the dimness,
providing the illusion of safety-

a smothering force,
a cocoon built to be kept small
to be kept
still.

Like a timid caterpillar,
destined for beauty,
a greatness seemingly too far.

Others knew their place, had a place,
found a place.
But what is a place
with an unknown purpose?

When the veil is worn and fragile,
dim light finds a way
to shine,
to call,
even beg- desperately pleading to stay.

No longer to be ignored,
no longer to be in doubt.

An outdated version feared these wings,
but they are bursting free-
now.

...

Wings so beautiful and vibrant
meant to take,
meant to make,
a life.

Growth becomes inevitable.
Transformation is the only way.
And when my wings blossom,
you'll be gone…

and left behind,
the old me
will
stay.

Time

Chasing time,
wasting time,
wishing for more-
but choosing to ignore.

Moments and minutes
continue to pass by
as you watch your life
flash in the blink of an eye.

What are you waiting for?

For those who have silently carried the weight of postpartum expectations- this is for you.

Enough

once you are here
everything changes
I change
I've waited for you
for this day
to become this person
yet
I don't know her
I can't believe you're mine
all tiny
soft and perfect
can I do this
I want to hold you
nurse you
be who I'm supposed
to be
do
what I'm made to do
but
you make it difficult
I try
anyway
hiding my fears
quieting my doubts
It will be easy
everyone says
but it's not
easy
and something is wrong

...

wrong with me
wrong with you
there is no separation
we rely on each other
I don't ask for help
because
this is my purpose
you need me
I don't ask for help,
because
they
didn't
you don't sleep when you
should
or eat *right*
the very purpose
of my body
fails me
fails you
I'm a
failure
insecure answers
to questions asked
no gut intuition
a mother
am I
I question myself
tears in the dark
behind
closed doors.
fake smiles
in daylight
though my heart
hurts
sheltered at home

...

where I don't have to lie
but sheltered
alone
my love for you
drives me
to the ends of
the earth
I will do anything
to make you
smile
to keep you
safe
yet my soul
feels depleted
why me
why us
your eyes look for me
in every room
in every space
you curl into my arms
fit into the
places
that comfort me
smile
when I smile
laugh
when I snuggle you
you have no doubts
my struggles are not yours
because
I am yours
and
to you
I am
enough

Shadows

You're always there,
lingering
in the depths of despair,
in the heart of repair.

You present yourself in
sunlight
only to dampen the glow,
to remind us you're here
always near.

The part of us we fear.

Not many look
you straight in the eye,
or are willing to try.
But we all have a shadow,
some darker than others-
most of us operating
undercover.

We can keep you,
if we choose,
but we will lose
who we could be
if we uncovered the layers
to see:

Shadows are just reflections
of past directions,
detours and decisions
that weren't always winning.

...

Hard truths and pain-
it's all one in the same.

Carry it, or set it free.
It's on us
who we
want
to
be.

don't look back
the past is not waiting
but the future is
and the present is impatient
for you to take it

One by One

One by one,
pieces fall,
people fall,
their insecurities
risk it all.

You change
into something new,
someone new.
And those
meant to stand by
you-
they leave you too.

Uncomfortable
in the discomfort
too beautiful for the naked eye,
your glimmer makes them
shiver,
makes them break down,
makes them cry.

But their tears never stop
you,
never floods the willpower
you hold.
Their obligations no longer fit
within
the spaces you provide.

The puzzle isn't fitting,
isn't living,

...

because your growing,
and it's showing-
and they can't handle
the ride

*the best of things are born in the silence
in the quiet created alone
inspired by beauty
nurtured through action
until they blossom
behind closed doors
and humble hearts*

The Becoming

The moment we remember we are not our fears, our doubts or our past. We rise, we become.
Braver, softer and more authentic than we've ever been.

Listen

Have you ever heard it?
The voice calling you home-

Do you stop and listen when it whispers,
do you give it space to be known?

A nudge that guides with
unwavering patience,
only relentless in your absence.

It resides in the rush of wind,
tousling your hair
awakening the fibers of your skin.

The gentle warmth of sun
bleeding into the air.

It opens in your mind.
In your heart.

And you must follow-
a swirling depth
in the core of your being.

When you know, you know.
And there is no denying
a gift from your soul.

The compass in your story,
navigating rough waters,
but never abandoning.

...

Stand at the edge
open your eyes.
Spread your arms,
and free fall.
It's got you.

alanaavellinoauthor | poetry

Growth

Strength grows
behind closed doors,
beneath the surface
of portrayal.

Quietly enduring
the mountain of life,
preserving
a lengthy battle.

The vision is yours.
The dream on your heart,
placed in your soul
for a reason.

In silence, you trek
through past and present,
embodying
a newly born season.

Growth goes unseen-
until
it's all that is seen.

Until reflections
only make you smile.
Until one day, it clicks.
Until one day, it fits.

Realizing the journey,
your journey-
was always
worthwhile.

Wake Up

Wake up-
the voice is always calling,
echoing
in dreams unknown.
Pulling you to safety,
guiding you
home.

Wake up-
your power lies within,
in the depths
of hearts and souls.
In the magnetic puzzle pieces,
the softness makes you whole.

Wake up-
there is no space for smallness.
It's inevitable.
Unstoppable.
Nothing will change its course,
when magic meets destiny
and becomes the driving force.

Wake up-
claim it,
with steady hands to hold
it's yours to keep,
to nurture.
A watered seed
will always grow.

...

Wake up-
and live your life
unapologetically,
authentically,
remembering who you are.

The rest is just background noise.
The risk is the reward.

Seed

A tiny seed
that blossoms in your mind,
uncontrollably cruel
until forced to be kind-
to be the kind of seed that grows
into a thought.

A thought of strength and power,
innate,
not taught.

But a seed that grows
thorns,
forces blood to spill,
forces beliefs against
your will.

Don't fall prey
to what is said to be true.
Nurture the power
that lies within
you.

Nurturing the mind
is how you
breakthrough.

when the past lingers don't be led astray
it's just residue that eventually washes away

Miracles

Magic happens beneath
the soil.
Blossoms bloom
in a quiet journey,
fed by power and light-

not to be watched,
or waited on,
but left in the silence
of expectation.

In the excitement of miracles.
In the beauty of life.
In the cycles that begin
and end.

Believe

Persistence in the face
of resistance-
trusting what cannot be seen,
felt in depths between your bones.
Only you know.
Showing up the way you
believe.

Chaos attempts to pull
you under.
Filter out doubts, shut down
the fear.
Life is a kaleidoscope of colour;
upheaval sometimes appears
when blessings are near.

Rejections will test you,
harden your heart.
Uncertainty creeps in
under your skin,
warning you
not to start.

But start as you may.
Believe what you must.
Let your soul be the guiding
force-
the pull
the trust.

Waiting

When we live in the waiting,
life becomes watching,
becomes impatient
and urgent.

Until life isn't living,
until living is just wishing
for what comes next,

forgetting that what is in front
of us
is truly life's
gift.

Patience

You cannot rush
what is not seen.
waiting is patience-
part of the recipe.

Not everyone has it,
a skill to pour into.
When you falter,
it falters
becoming
long overdue.

Detach from expectations,
focus on other inspirations,
broaden your horizons
and be surprised when
it arrives.
in ways you never imagined.

Patience turns to
trust,
turns to faith,
and knowing is
what ends up growing
your wishes
into
gifts.

Blessings

Who teaches us to hold it,
to receive and to know?
When it shows up big and grand,
with magic in hand-
a destined plan.

Unchartered waters
leave room for questions,
for second guessing,
forgetting this is fate.
This *is* the blessing.

The blessing dreamt about,
prayed for,
screamed and shouted
to whoever would listen.
And they listened.
And they heard
every tear and every word.

It's here for you to hold,
with gratitude and grace.
And all this time,
you've created space-
space for it to land,
for this version to take place,
for you to take the stand
in your life.

Faith

Never understanding
the blindness in trust.

The power in believing-
in knowing,
in dreaming
that it must
work out.

Must happen just so,
stretching and
flexing patience
isn't something we all
know.

Believing isn't seeing,
it's a deep-rooted feeling
that continues to call
on you-

in times of unrest,
in times when your trust
is put to the test.

When praying and saying
you'll do anything,

words do not hold the power
it's action within your soul,
a guiding light within
you
when you feel it,
you'll know.

...

When you begin to listen
and touch its safe embrace,
the blindness in believing
becomes
second nature.

*on the days when it's too much
feels too far close your eyes
and remember when you wished
for this moment
then remind yourself
you are capable*

Peace

Peace comes in waves,
in the days you take time
to admire.

The beauty of life is not just
in the breaths we take,
but in the subtle breeze
that caresses your cheek.

When sun warms your skin,
illuminating within
the essence of light.

Clean air that breathes
life.
Stars that dance in the blackest
of nights.

In the flutter of wings,
the song of all
things
that live on
and around us.

In the beauty of stillness
you see the living,
witness the universe
continue to give us
everything

take it in-
and be grateful.

Embers

Your beauty and strength
was born from a sacred place,
a place long forgotten in time.

After life happened fiercely,
you dimmed your light briefly,
but dreams continued calling
your name.

It's a power innate,
not meant for one place,
but to radiate all it
encompasses.

Magnified in loss,
through trials of pain,
growing forward in
expansion each day.

The embers within
a tiny flame-
burn,
spreading wildfire across
your soul,
burning to the ground
the old parts unfound,
reclaiming its place
once more.

If you made it to the end of this collection,
thank you.
Thank you for giving my words a place to land, a place to blossom and grow.
I hope something here has stayed with you:
a line,
a feeling,
a reminder that you are not alone.

Acknowledgements

To my family and friends- thank you for always encouraging me to share my words with the world. For reading my poems and drafts, sometimes daily, and responding with nothing but kindness. Your belief in me gave me the courage to do something I've dreamed of, for so long.

I am deeply grateful for each and every one of you. For your support, your love, and for holding space for my voice.

About the Author

Alana Avellino is a Canadian writer and poet whose work explores themes of identity, healing, becoming, and emotional resilience. *Dear Diary* is her debut poetry collection, born from years of journaling, deep feeling and a belief in the power of words.

Her poem *Becoming* will be published in the upcoming *Kaleidoscopic Quill: A Butterfly Anthology* by Wild Ink Publishing in March 2026. Alana is also currently working on her second collection *Love Letters to Myself* as well as a YA contemporary fiction novel that delves into grief, anxiety, love and the quiet strength of resilience.

Through her poetry and stories, she hopes to connect with readers who long to feel seen and understood.

Printed in Dunstable, United Kingdom